AN AMERICAN Thanksgiving

ideals®

AN AMERICAN
Thanksgiving

AMERICAN SAMPLERS by R. J. McGinnis, Reprinted with permission from *GOOD OLD DAYS* Magazine, 306 East Parr Rd., Berne, IN 46711; GOIN' HOME by Edna Jaques from her book *HILLS OF HOME*, copyright © 1946 by Thomas Allen and Son Publishers, Ltd.; THANKSGIVING DAY IN THE MORNING by Aileen Fisher. Copyrighted. Used by permission of the author; OCTOBER from *THE POETRY OF ROBERT FROST* edited by Edward Connery Lathem. Copyright 1934, © 1969 by Holt, Rinehart and Winston. Copyright © 1962 by Robert Frost. Reprinted by permission of Henry Holt and Company, Inc.; LET US NOT FORGET by Grace Noll Crowell. From *LET THE SUN SHINE IN* by Grace Noll Crowell, copyright 1970 by Fleming H. Revell Company. Used by permission; AUTUMN TIME by Edgar A. Guest. From *EDGAR A. GUEST BROADCASTING*, copyright 1935, the Reilly & Lee Co. Used by permission; TO WALK IN BEAUTY and THE TURKEY by Hal Borland. From *SUNDIAL OF THE SEASONS* by Hal Borland, published by J.B. Lippincott Co. Reprinted by permission of Frances Collin, Literary Agent. Copyright © 1964 by Hal Borland; TURKEY ONCE A YEAR by Gladys Taber. Specified excerpt from pp. 226-229 in *STILLMEADOW CALENDAR* by Gladys Taber (J.B. Lippincott Company). Copyright © 1967 by Gladys Taber. Reprinted by permission of Brandt & Brandt Literary Agents, Inc.; THE PILGRIMS FIRST THANKSGIVING MEAL by Margaret H. Koehler. (Originally titled: "Pilgrim Recipes") Adapted. From *EARLY AMERICAN LIFE* magazine, 1974. Reprinted with permission of the publisher; FEAST TIME OF THE YEAR author unknown. From *OUR HOLIDAYS IN POETRY*, compiled by Mildred P. Harrington and Josephine H. Thomas, published by the H.W. Wilson Company, New York, 1929.

ISBN 0-8249-4042-3

Published by Ideals Publications Incorporated
Nashville, Tennessee

Printed and bound in the United States of America.

TABLE OF CONTENTS

The Season of Thanksgiving

We Thank Thee

Ralph Waldo Emerson

For flowers that bloom about our feet;
For tender grass, so fresh, so sweet;
For song of bird, and hum of bee;
For all things fair we hear or see,
Father in heaven, we thank Thee!

For blue of stream and blue of sky;
For pleasant shade of branches high;
For fragrant air and cooling breeze;
For beauty of the blooming trees,
Father in heaven, we thank Thee!

Ode to Autumn

John Keats

Season of mists and mellow fruitfulness!
Close bosom-friend of the maturing sun;
Conspiring with him how to load and bless
With fruit the vines that round the thatch-eaves run;

To bend with apples the moss'd cottage trees,
And fill all fruit with ripeness to the core;
To swell the gourd, and plump the hazel shells
With a sweet kernel; to set budding more,
And still more, later flowers for the bees,
Until they think warm days will never cease,
For Summer has o'er-brimmed their clammy cells.

Who hath not seen thee oft amid thy store?
Sometimes whoever seeks abroad may find
Thee sitting careless on a granary-floor,
Thy hair soft lifted by the winnowing wind;
Or, on a half-reap'd furrow sound asleep,
Drowsed with the fume of poppies, while thy hook
Spares the next swath and all its twined flowers;

And sometimes like a gleaner thou dost keep
Steady thy laden head across a brook;
Or by a cider-press, with patient look,
Thou watchest the last oozings, hours by hours.

Where are the songs of Spring? Ay, where are they?
Think not of them; thou hast thy music, too,
While barred clouds bloom the soft-dying day,
And touch the stubble plains with rosy-hue;
Then in a wailful choir the small gnats mourn
Among the river swallows, borne aloft
Or sinking as the light wind lives or dies;
And full-grown lambs loud bleat from hilly bourn;
Hedge-crickets sing; and now with treble soft
The redbreast whistles from a garden croft,
And gathering swallows twitter in the skies.

Autumn Evening

Vincent Godfrey Burns

What magic there is in the wand
Which autumn wields
When it pours its stream of gold
On the harvest fields:
A loveliness tinting all
That shines to the eyes,
With purple curtains of haze
Let down from the skies;
The maples with flaming banners
In every wood,
The cornstalks like ranks
Of a rustic brotherhood;
The barns all bursting with grain
As the apples fall,
And a wondrous peace
Seems somehow part of it all.
There are rainbow colors
Mirrored in placid streams,
And earth seems hushed
To a music of whispers and dreams.
The bees are filling their hives
With a dusty gold,
And the heart is filled
With more than a heart can hold.

Thanksgiving Mural

Alice Leedy Mason

Create a mural with great expertise;
Paint scenes depicting Thanksgiving and Peace.

Start with a mountain, majestic and grand;
Drape it in mist like the palm of a hand.

Sketch in the bear, the eagle, the deer;
Wind little streamlets, icy and clear.

Plunge shaggy cliffs straight down as they go
Or drop a worn path toward the village below.

Show me a valley bursting its seams;
Paint in the harvest; lace it with streams.

Dapple with yellows; touch it with red;
Rustle the wings of wild geese overhead.

Find me a fence, split-rails asunder;
Nestle the crops from chill winds and thunder.

Dig me a well; construct a cool fountain;
Plant me some maples to color my mountain.

Place a stone seat by the mural and then
Teach me to share God's blessings with men.

To Walk in Beauty

Hal Borland

One now walks in Autumn itself, along the suburban street, beside the country road, in every woodland. For Autumn is the time of the fallen leaf, and the leaves are crispness underfoot, brown and red and yellow and sere tan, the leftover of summer shade, paper-thin jewel flakes that bring the sunlight and the vividness of sunset down to earth.

There was an old Navaho prayer song that said:

> Beauty before me, I return.
> Beauty above me, I return.
> Beauty below me, I return.
> Beauty all around me, with it I return.

It was a song of the Southwest, where the aspens are full of gold now and the scrub oak makes the foothills rich with wine; but we of the northeastern woodlands should know such a song, when Autumn comes down from the treetops. Beauty, the fragile but abundant beauty of the turning leaves, is before us, above us, below us, and all around us.

The birch leaves drift down at midday a sunny shower. The sugar maples are pure gold when dawn light strikes through them; and beneath them the rustling gold leaf begins to cover the grass. The swamp maples are cherry red, and knee-deep in their own color. The poplars stand naked in pools of tarnished gold, their leaves shed. The beeches are rustling with gilt glazes, to which they will cling for weeks to come. The oaks are leather-clad, russet and oxblood and purple and ruddy brown; brown as acorns, crisp as parchment.

One walks in Autumn, now, beauty above, below, and all around.

Thanksgiving

Jean M. Helferich

There dawned a frosty morning
In the autumn of the year,
When the crops had all been gathered,
And the air was crisp and clear.

The Pilgrims all rose early
To lend a helping hand
And lay a festive table
With the bounty of the land.

Soon the farmers from the harvest
And the hunters from the wood
Brought the pumpkins and the turkeys
And the ripened fruits they could.

Then the Pilgrims paused a moment,
To bow their heads and pray,
And thanked God for His blessings
On that first Thanksgiving Day.

To Walk with Autumn

Mildred L. Jarrell

I was alone with Autumn;
The country road was still.
I stood beneath the tinted trees;
The passing breeze was chill.

Crisp, curled leaves came drifting
To hide where deer-trails led;
Sunlight danced on bittersweet,
A brilliant orange red.

Sumac hugs the old stone fence
Where asters vie for space;
Swaying in drifting shafts of gold,
Hang spider webs of lace.

Over the browning meadow,
Beyond a brook's bright spill,
She deftly wrapped a hazy shawl
About the distant hill.

Soon in her waning hour,
Will come her closing song,
Echoed in wild geese calling
As they speed along.

I was alone with Autumn,
Wishing that I could keep
All of her flaming glory
As earth prepares for sleep.

Fall Is Settling Down

Craig E. Sathoff

When wheat fields turn to burnished dun—
That special shade of brown
That makes you think of fresh-baked buns—
Then fall is settling down.

When corn hangs heavy on its stalk,
When geese are on the wing,
When cabbage heads are center-split,
It's time for harvesting.

When canning and preserving crops
Have almost all been done
And carrots stored deep underground,
The fall is soon to come.

When cider making is in vogue
And quilts are back in style,
When footballs spiral through the air,
Fall's with us for a while.

A vibrant, restless air arrives
When leaves turn red and brown
And bonfires dot the countryside,
For fall is settling down.

A Poet's Thanksgiving

Selection

John Greenleaf Whittier

Heap high the farmer's wintry hoard!
Heap high the golden corn!
No richer gift has autumn poured
From out her lavish horn.

Let other lands exulting glean
The apple from the pine,
The orange from its glossy green,
The cluster from the vine.

But let the good old corn adorn
The hills our fathers trod;
Still let us, for his golden corn,
Send up our thanks to God.

October

Robert Frost

O hushed October morning mild,
Thy leaves have ripened to the fall;
Tomorrow's wind, if it be wild,
Should waste them all.
The crows above the forest call;
Tomorrow they may form and go.
O hushed October morning mild,
Begin the hours of this day slow.
Make the day seem to us less brief.
Hearts not averse to being beguiled,
Beguile us in the way you know.

Release one leaf at break of day;
At noon release another leaf;
One from our trees, one far away.
Retard the sun with gentle mist;
Enchant the land with amethyst.
Slow, slow!
For the grapes' sake, if they were all,
Whose leaves already are burnt with frost,
Whose clustered fruit must else be lost—
For the grapes' sake along the wall.

Autumn

Henry Wadsworth Longfellow

With what glory comes and goes the year!
The buds of spring, those beautiful harbingers
Of sunny skies and cloudless times, enjoy
Life's newness, and earth's garniture spread out;
And when the silver habit of the clouds
Comes down upon the autumn sun, and with
A sober gladness the old year takes up
His bright inheritance of golden fruits,
A pomp and pageant fill the splendid scene.
There is a beautiful spirit breathing now
Its mellow richness on the clustered trees.
And, from a beaker full of richest dyes,
Pouring new glory on the autumn woods,
And dipping in warm light the pillared clouds.
Morn on the mountain, like a summer bird,
Lifts up her purple wing, and in the vales
The gentle wind, a sweet and passionate wooer,
Kisses the blushing leaf and stirs up life
Within the solemn woods of ash, deep-crimsoned,
And silver beech and maple, yellow leaved,
Where autumn, like a faint old man, sits down
By the wayside a-weary. Through the trees
The golden robin moves. The purple finch,
That on wild cherry and red cedar feeds,
A winter bird, comes with its plaintive whistle,
And pecks by the witch hazel, whilst aloud,
From cottage roofs the warbling bluebird sings,
And merrily, with oft-repeated stroke,
Sounds from the threshing floor the busy flail.
Oh, what a glory doth this world put on
From him who, with a fervent heart, goes forth
Under the bright and glorious sky, and looks
On duties well performed and days well spent!

The Twilight of Thanksgiving

William D. Kelley

The day has lengthened into eve,
And over all the meadows
The twilight's silent shuttles weave
Their sombre web of shadows;
With northern lights the cloudless skies
Are faintly phosphorescent,
And just above yon wooded rise
The new moon shows her crescent.

Before the evening lamps are lit,
While day and night commingle,
The sire and matron come and sit
Beside the cozy ingle;
And softly speak of the delight
Within their bosoms swelling,
Because beneath their roof tonight
Their dear ones all are dwelling.

And when around the cheerful blaze
The young folks take their places,
What blissful dreams of other days
Light up their aged faces!

The past returns with all its joys,
And they again are living
The years in which, as girls and boys,
Their children kept Thanksgiving.

The stalwart son recalls the time
When, urged to the endeavor,
He tried the well-greased pole to climb,
And failed of fame forever.
The daughter tells of her emprise
When, as a new beginner,
She helped her mother make the pies
For the Thanksgiving dinner.

And thus with laugh and jest and song,
And tender recollections,
Love speeds the happy hours along,
And fosters fond affections;
While Fancy, listening to the mirth,
And dreaming pleasant fictions,
Imagines through the winds on earth
That heaven breathes benedictions.

Goin' Home

Edna Jaques

Goin' home—what lovelier word
Ever—ever—could be heard,
Home to warmth and firelight,
Little rooms that shine at night,
Back to the comfort of old things,
A kitchen where a kettle sings.

Goin' home—to supper spread,
Fried potatoes and homemade bread,
Slippers warm beside the hearth,
Loveliest spot in all the earth,
A new book and an easy chair,
Someone precious waiting there.

Goin' home—to the place you've made
With your own hands that you wouldn't trade
For a palace on a golden hill;
Where you've sweated and planned until
Every tree in the rooted soil
Is yours by dint of patient toil.

Goin' home—with heart aglow.
Down the old road white with snow.
There a lighted window gleams,
Sending out its golden beams
Like a lighthouse tall and white,
Shining out against the night.

Goin' home—what lovelier word
Ever—ever—has been heard?

Autumn Dancers

Craig E. Sathoff

The dancers on the water are
Bright colored leaves of fall
That float from trees which grace the shore
To join the festive ball.

The orchestra—a cricket's call,
A softly whispering breeze,
The cry of geese in southern flight,
The dove's deep tones of ease.

The dance— a jolly, spritely step
With sunbeams all about,
With dancers bowing gracefully
To partners they've sought out.

The mood is one of peacefulness
Of idling leaves of fall
That, drifting gently on the breeze,
Bring harmony to all.

Come Ye Thankful People

Henry Alford

George J. Elvey

1. Come, ye thank-ful peo - ple, come, Raise the song of har - vest home!
2. We our-selves are God's own field, Fruit un - to his praise to yield;
3. For the Lord our God shall come, And shall take his har - vest home;
4. E - ven so, Lord, quick-ly come, Bring thy fi - nal har - vest home;

All is safe - ly gath - ered in, Ere the win - ter storms be - gin;
Wheat and tares to - geth - er sown Un - to joy or sor - row grown;
From his field shall purge a - way All that doth of - fend that day;
Gath - er thou thy peo - ple in, Free from sor - row, free from sin;

God, our Mak - er, doth pro - vide For our wants to be sup - plied:
First the blade, and then the ear, Then the full corn shall ap - pear;
Give his an - gels charge at last In the fire the tares to cast;
There, for - ev - er pu - ri - fied, In thy pres - ence to a - bide;

Come to God's own tem - ple, come, Raise the song of har - vest home.
Lord of har - vest! grant that we Wholesome grain and pure may be.
But the fruit - ful ears to store In his gar - ner ev - er - more.
Come, with all thine an - gels, come, Raise the glo - rious har - vest home.

'Tis Autumn Again

Garnett Ann Schultz

A whispering breeze,
A bright touch of gold,
Some frost on the window,
A day fair and cold;
Some red and some orange,
A soft gentle rain,
The leaves softly falling—
'Tis autumn again.

A trace still of green.
A quiet to keep,
The flowers of springtime.
At last fast asleep;
One moment of winter,
Leaves deep in the lane,
We tuck away summer—
'Tis autumn again.

An Historic Thanksgiving

America's First Official Thanksgiving

hether you choose to celebrate the arrival of Thanksgiving Day with prayers, family feasts, parades, or football games you will no doubt agree that the American celebration of this holiday began with an intrepid group of Pilgrims at Plymouth, Massachusetts in the year 1620.

Or did it? Thanksgiving celebrations in cultures around the world are as old as recorded history, dating back to the Hebrews, Greeks, and Romans, and Thanksgiving—American-style—actually began before the Pilgrims boarded the *Mayflower.*

In 1619, Captain John Woodlief set sail on the tiny ship *Margaret* with a small band of followers and specific instructions from the London Company, which stated in part: "Wee ordaine the day of our ship's arrival at the place assigned for plantacon in the land of Virginia shall be yearly and perpetually keept holy as a day of Thanksgiving to Almighty God."

The *Margaret* landed at Jamestown and laid claim to a very choice piece of property: eight thousand acres of meadowland and virgin forests with three miles of riverfront. There, after coming ashore on an early December day in 1619, the small company knelt on the dried grass to pray.

With thanks given to God, the members of the company set about building their new home. By the time the *Margaret* left in January, a storehouse, an assembly hall, and several crude homes were already constructed and over the years, the settlement, which was known as "Berkeley Hundred," grew to become one of the premier plantations of the South.

Although few would dispute the historic significance of the Pilgrims at Plymouth, President John F. Kennedy, in an official Thanksgiving Proclamation, recognized Virginia's contribution when he declared: "Over three centuries ago, our forefathers in Virginia and Massachusetts, far from home in a lonely wilderness, set aside a time of thanksgiving. On that appointed day they gave reverent thanks for their safety, for the health of their children, for the fertility of their fields, for the love which bound them together, and for the faith which united them with God." Today, visitors to Berkeley Hundred can tour the historic buildings and grounds and relive the landing of the *Margaret* and America's first Thanksgiving celebration. The official re-enactment is held yearly on the first Sunday in November.

The Journey of the *Mayflower*

Linda Robinson

In the early seventeenth century, a group of English religious dissenters immigrated to Holland seeking a place to worship freely. Not long after their arrival in Leyden, Netherlands, however, a fear of losing their religious freedom arose again after the dissolution of a truce between the Netherlands and Spain. This prompted the famous voyage which brought the Pilgrims to America.

Various agreements authorizing settlement and assurance of free worship were made with the Virginia Company of London, while principle funding was obtained through a group of London merchants. A ship called the *Speedwell* carried the Pilgrims to southern England, where they joined their chartered ship, the *Mayflower*. The *Speedwell* was to accompany the *Mayflower*, but a succession of leaks caused her to remain in England. The *Mayflower* set out alone for the northern coast of Virginia on September 6, 1620, with nearly one hundred men, women, and children aboard.

The twelve-year-old *Mayflower,* under the direction of Captain Christopher Jones, was known as a "sweet ship," meaning that her previous wine cargoes left a scent which somewhat detracted from the unpleasant atmosphere. Ninety feet in length, she was capable of carrying 180 tons. Thanks to William Bradford, principle leader and historian for the Pilgrims, we have some record of the journey. A general state of discomfort as a result of overcrowding, dampness, and cold prevailed throughout the trip, which was hampered by storms and strong winds. After two months on the open sea, land was sighted; however, it was to be another month before the small crew aboard a shallop would go ashore and explore the new land. The voyage had been a good one in spite of the season, and the *Mayflower* anchored herself in what is now Provincetown Harbor, waiting for a go-ahead from the shallop crew.

The actual significance of Plymouth Rock has been disputed. Did the first exploring party land there? Or did it mark a beachhead, later developed into a wharf? The Rock was not mentioned in Bradford's writings. It was identified as the landing place of the Pilgrims by Thomas Faunce, last Ruling Elder of the Plymouth Church; this knowledge had been forwarded to him by his father, who arrived in Plymouth via the ship *Anne* in 1623.

Through the years, Plymouth Rock has been moved to various places, but today it finally rests near its original place, somewhat protected from the action of the sea, yet lapped by the waves in its historic setting. As a national symbol, Plymouth Rock commemorates the important voyage of our forefathers, who crossed the Atlantic seeking freedom in a new and strange land.

The Landing

Felicia D. Hemans

The breaking waves dashed high
On a stern and rock-bound coast,
And the woods against a stormy sky
Their giant branches tossed;

And the heavy night hung dark
The hills and waters o'er,
When a band of exiles moored their bark
On the wild New England shore.

Not as the conqueror comes,
They, the true-hearted came;
Not with the roll of the stirring drums,
And the trumpet that sings of fame:

Not as the flying come,
In silence and in fear;
They shook the depths of the desert gloom
With their hymns of lofty cheer.

Amidst the storm they sang,
And the stars heard, and the sea;
And the sounding aisles of the dim woods rang
To the anthem of the free.

The ocean eagle soared
From his nest by the white wave's foam,
And the rocking pines of the forest roared—
This was their welcome home.

There were men with hoary hair
Amidst that Pilgrim band:
Why had they come to wither there,
Away from their childhood land?

There was woman's fearless eye,
Lit by her deep love's truth;
There was manhood's brow serenely high,
And the fiery heart of youth.

What sought they thus afar?
Bright jewels of the mine?
The wealth of seas, the spoils of war?
They sought a faith's pure shrine!

Ay, call it holy ground,
The soil where first they trod;
They have left unstained what there they found,
Freedom to worship God.

The First Presidential
Thanksgiving Proclamation

George Washington proclaimed the first official national Thanksgiving Day in his first year as president. In his proclamation, he cited the nationwide peace and the ratification of the Constitution as causes for gratitude, and declared the third Thursday in November of 1789 as a day of solemn celebration of the blessings bestowed upon the new American nation:

> *I do recommend and assign Thursday, the twenty-sixth of November next, to be devoted by the people of these states to the service of that great and glorious Being . . . for the signal and manifold mercies, and the favorable interpositions of his providence in the course and conclusion of the late war; for the great degree of tranquility, union, and plenty, which we have since enjoyed; for the peaceable and rational manner in which we have been enabled to establish Constitutions of Government for our safety and happiness . . .*

Over the next few decades, only Presidents John Adams and James Madison proclaimed national Thanksgiving celebrations. The other presidents left the decision about a Thanksgiving Day to the governors of each state, keeping the presidency out of the still-active debate over the right of a civil government to proclaim a national religious holiday.

Plymouth Rock

More likely than not, the Pilgrims did not actually land on Plymouth Rock, although they would certainly have noticed the ten-ton boulder as they approached land. After a two-month journey across a vast and furious ocean, they were discouraged by their arrival on the bleak New England coastline. Too late in the season to plant crops, and with the long winter ahead, they had no friends to welcome them—only a desolate and unknown wilderness. In order to help guide them through the surely difficult times ahead, the Pilgrims drew up the now-famous Mayflower Compact. An important part of our American heritage, the Compact authorized the election of the first colonial governor in the New World by the colonists themselves, rather than his appointment by the King or Council.

Long and difficult years were to come and pass before it became certain that the Plymouth colony would survive. For the eventual survivors, to have landed and to have endured was enough; where they landed was of interest to almost no one. But nearly a century and a half later, descendants of Plymouth's first settlers organized the Old Colony Club. They voted to commemorate "the landing of our worthy ancestors" each year by observing Forefather's Day, which is still celebrated on December twenty-first. It was at one such occasion, around the year 1770, that Deacon Ephraim Spoon first revealed to the club members a story of the ancestral landing on Plymouth Rock as it had been related from one generation of his family to the next since 1620.

The legend grew, and with it grew the rock's symbolic value. Just before the Revolutionary War, a group known as the Sons of Liberty attempted to move the rock from its place at the wharf which had been constructed over it in 1741. As they pulled it from the harbor, the rock split in two. The top section was carted to the Town Square, where it remained for many years. Such famous men as John Quincy Adams and Daniel Webster gave speeches at the site, expounding on the rock's symbolic meaning. Unfortunately, while the rock increased in fame, it began to decrease in size as people broke off fragments for souvenirs. Plymouth Rock was moved again in 1834; this time, it fell to the street and once more broke into two pieces. Meanwhile the bottom section remained at the wharf, little noticed under the wheels of passing carts.

In 1880, the upper part was finally moved to join the lower in its original location at the waterfront. In 1920, for the 300th anniversary of the landing of the Pilgrims, the wharf was torn down and the site excavated to sea level. At last Plymouth Rock was together in one piece, located where it could once again be lapped by the high tide of the Atlantic.

The Original Thanksgiving Meal

James W. Hyland III

Our harvest being gotten in, our Governor sente four men out fowling that so we might, after a more special manner, rejoyce together after we had gathered the fruit of our labours. These four, in one day, killed as much fowl as, with a little help besides, served the company almost a week, at which time, amongst other recreations, we exercised our armes, many of the Indians coming amongst us.

And amongst the rest, their greatest King, Massasoit, with some ninety men, whom, for three days, we entertained and feasted.

And they went out and killed five deer, which they brought to the Plantation, and bestowed on our Governor and upon the Captaine and others.

And although it be not always so plentiful as it was at this time with us, yet, by the goodness of God, we are so farr from want that we often wish you partakers of our plentie.

Edward Winslow,
Plymouth, Massachusetts, 1621

What was the original Thanksgiving meal really like? It is surprising to learn that although many of our traditional Thanksgiving dishes are associated with the Pilgrims, most of these foods were not actually present at the original Thanksgiving meal. In fact, the entire Thanksgiving feast has changed substantially as it has evolved into the holiday we now celebrate.

History tells us that the original celebration lasted three days. Although the actual dates of the festival were never recorded, most historians agree that the event took place in October rather than November.

The occasion was an outdoor event, celebrated during one of New England's mild Indian summers. Sporting events such as shooting contests and other recreations were held between meals. The cooking was done on open spits and in outdoor ovens. Tables were made by placing long boards over sawhorses. Chairs consisted of stools and tree stumps. Eating utensils consisted primarily of pewter dishes, wooden bowls, knives, and spoons. (Forks were not commonly used in the seventeenth century.)

Because the feasting lasted for three days, a large number of ingredients went into the meals to add variety; they did not spend the last two days eating turkey leftovers! What they did and did not eat may come as a revelation.

Contrary to popular belief, turkey was probably not the main meat dish at the first

Thanksgiving. Turkeys are not even mentioned in the feast records; however, prior to the celebration, Governor Bradford had sent out four men to go fowling. The records state that "these four, in one day, killed as much fowl as served the company almost a week." We can assume that turkeys were among the birds killed, as they were very plentiful in the region. The Pilgrims had taken in a "great store of wild Turkies" during the summer. However, duck and goose must also be added to the list of original ingredients in the American Thanksgiving meal. Records show that these fowl were also plentiful.

Perhaps the largest single meat dish was venison, as Chief Massasoit and his braves brought five deer to the feast for their contribution to the meal. Other meats at the banqueting table included striped bass, cod, lobster, eel, clams, and other shellfish. With such a wide array of meats and seafood, twentieth-century cooks can choose from a large selection of main dishes and still serve what could be called—technically—a very "traditional" Thanksgiving meal!

Old and New World vegetables provided a delightful mixture to the first menu. These included beans, pumpkins, squash, turnips, parsnips, barley, onions, leeks, watercress and other "sallet herbes," and roasted Indian corn (the colorful variety we now hang on our doors and lampposts in autumn). A small amount of peas may also have been included. (Unfortunately, the pea crop had largely failed that year. Letters to England reveal that despite an abundant corn harvest, "the peas (were) not worth gathering, for we feared they were too late sown. They came up very well and blossomed, but the sun parched them in the blossom.")

White and dark breads were served with butter during the feast. The white bread consisted of leftover ship biscuit (and butter) from the *Mayflower*. The dark bread was made of cornmeal, barley, and rye flour. It was called "Rye and Injun" and was very nutritious. It soon became the common bread of the early colonists.

Wild fruits grew in abundance in the American wilderness. Among those fruits that graced the first Thanksgiving table were wild plums and dried wild blueberries, blackberries, raspberries, and strawberries. A popular misconception is that the Pilgrims also ate cranberries. Although neighboring bogs were full of them, there is no historical evidence that the Pilgrims ever learned to make use of the red fruit that would later become one of the area's leading industries.

Fruits served as the primary dessert fare on the original Thanksgiving menu. There is a good chance, however, that hasty pudding or Indian pudding made from cornmeal was also served. Pumpkin pie, that all-American favorite Thanksgiving dessert, had not yet been invented. In the early days, the Pilgrims stewed their pumpkin and served it as a sauce. Their only pies were English-style meat pies. References indicate that succulent eel pie was among the items served during the original feast.

With its early origins on the shores of the American wilderness, our Thanksgiving is certainly the oldest and most distinctively American holiday that we celebrate as a people. And though the specifics of the celebration have changed through the years, the spirit of Thanksgiving remains true to that which inspired our original settlers to break from their routine for three days of feasting and celebration to give thanks for the blessings in their lives.

Thanksgiving at Old Sturbridge Village

Michael and Caroline Manheim

Thanksgiving Day finds an extra bustling in the crisp November air at Old Sturbridge Village, as the preparation of a feast is added to other activities of the season. It smells like Thanksgiving inside the Stephen Fitch House, where cranberry sauce is being prepared; at the John Fenno House, where a mincemeat pie is cooking; and at other locations throughout the village museum. An educational link with the past rides the air as easily as the aromas.

"But where's the turkey?" asks a puzzled young visitor to the General Salem Towne House. He had entered a kitchen filled with the fragrance of roasting turkey, but no bird is hanging over the blazing fire. An interpreter shows him how to lift the lid of a tin bake oven, situated a foot or two in front of the fireplace. Inside the oven a turkey is browning, and the interpreter, a woman dressed in period clothing who looks as though she actually lives in the house, turns a spit to keep the roasting even.

Old Sturbridge Village is a recreated community of the 1790 to 1840 era, with approximately forty structures located on 200 acres of farmland surrounding the Quinebaug River in the town of Sturbridge, Massachusetts. The Village opened in 1946.

A focal point of the living museum is the grassy Village Common ringed by a variety of buildings, including a towering Meetinghouse at one end and the imposing General Salem Towne Mansion at the other.

A horse drawn "carryall" offers free rides to those who want to climb aboard its benches. One trip starts near the Common, below the Tavern, and goes through woodlands to the Moses Wilder Blacksmith Shop. Inside the granite building a blacksmith pumps his bellows to fan a fire and heat up some metal. He might have been hammering out nails yesterday, showing and telling how each nail was hand-formed from an iron rod. Today the blacksmith demonstrates the forging of spits for bake ovens.

From outside the shop comes the sound of gunfire. At closer inspection you can see farmers using antique flintlock firearms in a demonstration of a wild turkey shoot. To add to the aura, a plucked turkey, ready for dressing for the bake oven, is hanging from an adjacent tree. Inside a farmhouse the women are roasting other turkeys and creating a Thanksgiving dinner that includes stuffing, vegetables, puddings, and pies.

Around noon the farm hands troop in, fill up their plates, and go off to enjoy their feast. A welcome respite from the day's chores, this Thanksgiving dinner is practical reinforcement of the importance of the domestic arts of the era.

Late in the afternoon many people gather in the Village Meetinghouse which functioned as both the seat of town government and a place of worship. Visitors attend a nonsectarian vesper service in the glow of candles burning in chandeliers. The atmosphere of the services provides a fitting ending to Thanksgiving Day, as Old Sturbridge Village shares with visitors its visions of yesteryear.

America's First National Thanksgiving Day

Today, we look upon Thanksgiving as a day to count our blessings and to share good times and good food with our families and friends, a day that is an accepted and treasured part of American life. But it has not always been this way. In fact, Thanksgiving was once considered quite controversial and has had to overcome opposition from members of Congress and an American president who believed that the government had no place in declaring or promoting this religious holiday. But through the controversy, the changes in style, and changes in date, the basic spirit of Thanksgiving has survived.

The origins of Thanksgiving go far back into ancient times. While today we think of Thanksgiving as a religious holiday, its roots are in the "harvest" celebrations of cultures around the world. The Chinese had a celebration thousands of years ago called the Moon Festival. This festival marked the end of the harvest season and was celebrated with special candies and cakes baked in the shape of the moon. Music, feasts and games highlighted the day.

European harvest festivals also have a long and varied history. In Austria, November fifteenth is known as St. Leopold's Day, or "Goose Day." On this day each year, lavishly prepared goose dinners hail the beginning of the new wine season. Historically, people have traveled to the Klosterneuburge Abbey (built in the twelfth century) to slide down the giant 12,000 gallon wine cask in an annual ritual of good luck. Germany's famous Octoberfest, known around the world for its merrymaking and tempting arrays of food and drink, also celebrates the harvest. Other European countries, such as Poland, use the corn maiden as their harvest symbol.

But what about America's turkey? How did this bird, often mistaken for an oversized chicken, become the center of our own harvest celebration? The turkey is a well traveled bird. Originally native to Mexico and the American Southwest, it was most likely taken to Spain by early explorers. From there, it is assumed that a few birds made their way to Turkey where they eventually became domesticated. Years later, possibly on a return trip with other explorers, the turkey found its way back to North America. As with the other customs of the day, even the dinner has somewhat confused origins.

The history of Thanksgiving in America traces back to those harsh times when the first settlers arrived. The Pilgrims' first winter was filled with hardship and sickness. Forty-seven of the *Mayflower*'s one hundred and three passengers succumbed. But with spring came planting and renewed hope. And also with that first spring came a Native American named Squanto, who befriended the Pilgrims and taught them how to plant and cultivate crops, including barley, peas and most importantly, corn.

After a spring and summer of hard work and hopeful prayer, the fall came, and the harvest. Although not bountiful, the yield of new crops was certainly plentiful. The Pilgrims had survived nearly a full year; and with the success of their first growing season, their further survival seemed assured. It seemed appropriate, thus, to set aside a day for celebration, and Governor William Bradford issued the following proclamation:

To All Ye Pilgrims:

Inasmuch as the great Father has given us this year an abundant harvest of Indian corn, wheat, beans, squashes, and garden vegetables, and has made the forests to abound with game and the sea with fish and clams, and inasmuch as He has protected us from the ravages of the savages, has spared us from pestilence and disease, has granted us freedom to worship God according to the dictates of our own conscience; now, I, your magistrate, do proclaim that all ye Pilgrims, with your wives and little ones, do gather at ye meeting house, on ye hill, between the hours of 9 and 12 in the day time, on Thursday, November ye 29th of the year of our Lord one thousand six hundred and twenty-three, and the third year since ye Pilgrims lande . . . there to listen to ye pastor, and render thanksgiving to ye Almighty God for all His blessings.

William Bradford
Governor

Over the years, Thanksgiving Day's march toward national acceptance has been hindered and delayed by the potholes of national discontent. President Jefferson maintained that Thanksgiving was becoming overtly religious and refused to proclaim a national Thanksgiving Day. In 1863, President Lincoln, during a year bloodied by the battles of Gettysburg and Vicksburg, gave into the impassioned pleas of one very persistent woman, Sara Hale, and issued his first Thanksgiving Day proclamation to hold the holiday on the last Thursday in November. President Franklin D. Roosevelt moved the holiday back a week out of consideration to Christmas shoppers. After several years of confusion, Congress passed a resolution legalizing the fourth Thursday in November as national Thanksgiving Day.

Nothing worthwhile comes easy; a day set aside to thank the Lord for blessings has been fraught with turmoil. But through it all, has survived. God willing, some form of giving thanks will always be a part of our national heritage.

AN HISTORIC THANKSGIVING

An Artist's Thanksgiving

The Feast Time of Year

Author Unknown

This is the feast time of the year,
When plenty pours her wine of cheer,
And even humble boards may spare
To poorer poor a kindly share.

While bursting barns and granaries know
A richer, fuller overflow,
And they who dwell in golden ease
Blessed without toil, yet toil to please.

This is the feast time of year,
The blessed Advent draweth near;
Rich and poor together break
The bread of love for Christ's sweet sake,

Against the time when rich and poor
Must ope for Him a common door
Who comes a guest, yet makes a feast,
And bids the greatest and the least.

Let Us Not Forget

Grace Noll Crowell

We should observe this day with more than feasting.
It should be one of gratitude and prayer
To the Author of all good, a day of praising
For the blessings that surround us everywhere.
A voice sounds from the wilderness as clearly
As when the words were uttered long ago,
"We will set a day aside for our thanksgiving
To God for the increase of the seeds we sow.
For his constant care that ever is about us;
For the promise of this new and untried land,
We will be grateful to Him for the mercies
That flow unhindered from His outflung hand."

Within our wilderness today, so should we
Be reverent and mindful as were they
Who faced each threatening danger, meeting bravely
The hardships they encountered day by day.
No less than theirs, our future is uncertain.
Today of all days, facing paths untrod,
May we not fail in gratitude for blessings
That are bestowed upon us by our God.

The Joy of Homecoming
in Durrie's "Home to Thanksgiving"

Mary Carolyn McKee

"Home to Thanksgiving," the print produced by Currier & Ives more than a century ago, is probably the most popular nineteenth-century picture of American life ever published by the famous New York lithographers. It presents a typical farm scene in old New England. An ox-drawn sledge stacked with logs stands in the barnyard and a small dog frolics nearby. At the front door of the farmhouse, the family welcomes a holiday guest arriving in a one-horse cutter. The home and farm buildings, as well as the haystack and hills in the background, are blanketed in snow.

George Henry Durrie was born June 6, 1820, in New Haven, Connecticut. His father was a bookseller and his mother, of Puritan stock, was a descendant of Governor William Bradford of Massachusetts.

jobs, such as touching up portraits, varnishing, and even painting window shades.

Soon they settled in New Haven, where Durrie announced his availability in a town newspaper, stating that "he would be pleased to wait upon those who may be desirous of obtaining faithful and correct likenesses." While he was painting tiny children, young folks, and their elders, he was carefully observing the beauty of rural areas—particularly during the winter season. On long walks, he would often stop to study the details of a door, a tree, a farmyard, or a stone wall. In his journal of January 1845, he noted that ice-covered trees glittering in the sun made a scene that was "almost enchanting." He was enthusiastic about the joy of sleighing along snowy winter roads. His love affair with winter was progressing! He exhibited his first two "snow pieces" at the New Haven Horticultural Society, then the painting "The Sleighing Party" at the National Academy Exhibit in New York City.

By 1854 he had produced so many winter scenes that he held a public sale of them, in sizes suited to the parlor or drawing room, for "admirers of the fine arts." "It is needless to add" said an advertisement in the New Haven *Register*, "that no collection of pictures is complete without one or more winter scenes."

About 1857 Durrie established contact with Currier & Ives, whose prints were fast building a rich panorama of American life. This was an exciting period for Durrie because he realized that he could bypass portraiture and concentrate on his beloved snow scapes. He was a fortunate man who had come into his own.

It may well be that the perennial popularity of Durrie's "Home to Thanksgiving" is connected to our nostalgic yearning for a simpler life. This painting captures—for all time—the quaint simplicity of a holiday on an old New England farm.

Durrie studied with Nathaniel Joselyn, a widely-known portrait painter, then launched into a career as a traveling portrait artist in New Jersey, New York, and Virginia, as well as in his native Connecticut.

While painting family portraits, the artist usually lived with the family. While in Bethany, Connecticut, at a church choir rehearsal, he met Sarah Perkins, the lovely daughter of "Squire" Perkins. They were married in the autumn of 1841.

His wife accompanied him on a number of portrait assignments; those were happy days for the young couple, although the family purse was often rather slim. Durrie augmented their modest income with odd

AN ARTIST'S THANKSGIVING

Prayer of Thanks

Eleanor Lyons Culver

Father please accept our thanks today
As round this table here we pause to pray;
Grateful hearts are warmed as we recall
'Tis from Thy bounty that our blessings fall.
This gladsome feast with loved ones now to share
Is but a measure of Thy tender care.

JOHN SLOBODNIK

AN ARTIST'S THANKSGIVING

Thanksgiving Hymn

Author Unknown

O thou, whose eye of love
Looks on us from above
Low at thy throne
We come to thee and pray
That, gleaning day by day,
Our grateful hearts always
Thy hand may own.

Thine are the waving fields,
Thy hand the harvest yields;
And unto thee
To whom for rain and dew,
And skies of sunny blue,
Our love and praise are due,
We bend the knee.

And when beneath the trees
In fairer fields than these
Our glad feet roam,
There where the bright harps ring,
May we our gleanings bring,
And in thy presence sing
Our harvest home.

Thanksgiving Grace

Louise Darcy

O Lord, we know that all things come from Thee
And as we bow our heads upon this day,
Thanking Thee for another harvest yield,
Our gratitude is boundless as we pray.

Lord of all life, we know Thy mighty hand
Encircles everyone throughout the year.
With deep devotion now we offer up
The thankful homage of those gathered here.

Harvest and Thanksgiving Time

Loise Pinkerton Fritz

I see a harvest moon tonight,
Though it's Thanksgiving time;
Its golden beams are shining still
On woodland's towering pines.
It shines upon the empty fields
Which have been harvested
And sheds a special ray of light
Upon the old homestead.

Again I see a harvest moon,
Though it's Thanksgiving time;
I feel a surge of thankfulness
Within this heart of mine.
The gathered fruit, heads bowed in prayer;
Where's one, we find the other;
For harvest and Thanksgiving time
Are kin to one another.

A Traditional Thanksgiving

The Thanksgiving Turkey

Hal Borland

That big, colorful, and meaty bird which makes the table annually festive for America's traditional Thanksgiving is surrounded by strange and contradictory legends. It is an American native, unknown elsewhere until the sixteenth century. It is generally believed that the name "turkey" came from the early discoverers' belief that the America they found was Asia; but logically, even under that misapprehension, the bird should have been called a Cathay hen. Confusion persisted when it received its scientific name, Meleagris. Meleagris literally means "guinea hen," a bird with no relation to the turkey.

The natives of Mexico and the Southwest had domesticated the turkey long before the Spaniards came, but in the Southwest it was grown for its feathers, not its flesh. The Spaniards took turkeys back to Spain, and thence they were distributed throughout Europe. Early English settlers brought turkeys to New England, only to find the woods full of wild turkeys. Later, when a national bird was being chosen, Ben Franklin and others urged the turkey for that honor. They lost the fight to the bald eagle.

The wild turkey, the deer, and the buffalo sustained most of the pioneers as the frontier moved west. And the turkey, deprived of formal honors, eventually ran away with the November holiday.

Even there it comes to an ironic fate, colorful with cranberries, savory with sage, tasty with stuffing and gravy and mashed potatoes and, if you will, onions and turnips, mincemeat, and pumpkin. The turkey, the all-American bird, provider of feathers and feasts, misnamed and imported to the land of its origins, symbol now of Thanksgiving. Long may the turkey gobble!

Over the River and through the Wood

LYDIA MARIA CHILD

TRADITIONAL

O- ver the riv- er and through the wood to Grand - fa- ther's house we go;___ the
O- ver the riv- er and through the wood, now soon we'll be on our way,___ there's

horse knows the way to car-ry the sleigh through the white and drift - ed snow.___
feast - ing and fun for ev__ 'ry one, for this is Thanks- giv - ing Day,___

O- ver the riv - er and through the wood, oh how the wind does blow!___ It
O- ver the riv - er and through the wood, get on, my dap - ple grey,___ the

stings the toes and bites the nose as o - ver the ground we go.
woods will ring with songs we sing, for this is Thanks - giv - ing Day.

The Pilgrim Forefathers

Helen Hunt Jackson

Neath hoary moss on crumbling stones
Their names are fading day by day;
The fashions of their lives and speech
From sight and sound are passed away.

The shores they found so bleak and bare
Shine now with riches gay and proud;
And we, light-hearted, dance on ground
Where they in anguish wept and bowed.

Unto the faith they bought so dear
We pay each day less reverent heed;
And boast, perhaps, that we outgrow
The narrowness that marked their creed.

A shallow boast of thankless hearts
In evil generations born;
By side of those old Pilgrim men
The ages shall hold us in scorn.

Find me the men on earth who care
Enough for faith or creed today
To seek a barren wilderness
For simple liberty to pray.

Men who for simple sake of God
All titles, riches, would refuse,
And in their stead disgrace and shame
And bitter poverty would choose.

We find them not. Alas! the age
In all its light hath blinder grown;
In all its plenty, starves because
It seeks to live by bread alone.

We owe them all we have of good;
Our sunny skies, our fertile fields,
Our freedom, which to all oppressed
A continent of refuge yields;

And what we have of ill, of shame,
Our broken word, our greed for gold,
Our reckless schemes and treacheries,
In which men's souls are bought and sold.

All these have come because we left
The paths that those forefathers trod;
The simple, single-hearted ways
In which they feared and worshiped God.

Despise their narrow creed who will!
Pity their poverty who dare!
Their lives knew joys, they wore crowns
We do not know, we cannot wear.

And if so be that it is saved,
Our poor republic, stained and bruised,
'Twill be because we lay again,
Their cornerstones which we refused.

Pumpkin Pie

*T*ake a common fall vegetable—and not a very attractive one at that—peel it, cook it, and puree it into a soupy mush. Season it with ginger, cloves, and nutmeg. Sweeten it with brown sugar, add a few more ingredients for tradition's sake, and pour it all into a simple crust. Then slide it into the oven and before long, the familiar, tantalizing aroma of pumpkin pie will pervade the kitchen and slowly make its way into adjoining rooms.

Topped with a bit of fresh whipped cream and maybe a sprinkling of pecans, or served alone alongside a hot cup of coffee, a homemade pumpkin pie is truly a dessert worth giving thanks for each November.

Pumpkin pie in its present form was most likely not served at the original Thanksgiving dinner, but the Pilgrims had already developed a taste for the pumpkin, as this early American verse attests:

> For pottage and puddings,
> And custards and pies,
> Our pumpkins and parsnips
> Are common supplies.
> We have pumpkins at morning
> And pumpkins at noon;
> If it were not for pumpkins,
> We should be undoon.

The Pilgrims' First Thanksgiving Meal

Margaret H. Koehler

*F*ew of us would attempt to duplicate the exact conditions under which the Pilgrims cooked the first Thanksgiving dinner. Yet we have made traditional some of the foods they used, even though they were using them from necessity, rather than choice. Their turkeys were wild; ours are almost excessively domesticated. But still the turkey spells Thanksgiving for most of us, as do cranberries. It would be just as authentic to include pickled herring and eel on the Thanksgiving table, though a nationwide poll would probably prove that few of us do.

Another dish that was probably a Pilgrim favorite was baked pumpkin. The recipe, which was originally borrowed from the Indians, called for a whole pumpkin, baked with the seeds still inside. The seeds were then removed and honey, butter, and apple cider spooned into the cavity. The pumpkin was then baked again to blend flavors. It was taken to the table whole and served by scooping out the meat.

Most of us think of succotash as a combination of lima beans and corn, mixed in equal parts and seasoned with salt, pepper and butter, but the Pilgrims, who learned about succotash from the Indians, used pea beans in the making of it; these are the same kind of beans we use in making New England baked beans today. Often, they cooked the corn and the beans with a chunk of meat, sometimes adding a chicken to the pot, thus making a hearty meal indeed. They were pioneers in the use of frozen foods, freezing dishes like this in the winter, then chopping off as much as was needed for a meal.

Although the meal served at the first Thanksgiving may not have been better than the delicious Thanksgiving fare we enjoy today, it certainly must have been different.

Give Me a Grateful Heart, Lord

Grace E. Easley

Give me a grateful heart, Lord
For each small favor granted.
As years unfold, may I behold
Life, still, through eyes enchanted.
Let me find beauty in all things,
Not be too blind to see
The goodness in my fellowman,
That he would find in me.

Grant that my ears remain attuned
To hear the smallest sigh,
And may I lend a gentle touch,
To those less sure than I.
Let me remember lessons learned,
To profit from the past,
And may I build a bridge of dreams,
That shall forever last.

Let me rejoice in simple things;
I need no wealth to buy
The scent of pine upon the wind,
A burnished copper sky,
Scarlet roses on the fence,
Sunrise through the trees—
Oh, grant that I may not outgrow
Affinity for these!

Give me a grateful heart, Lord;
Let me be satisfied
When days are less than sunny
And plans lie at low tide.
Life is a sweet adventure
That will lead to who knows where,
So, give me a grateful heart, Lord,
That I may always care.

Turkey Once a Year

Gladys Taber

When the children come for Thanksgiving, out comes the big roaster. Dinner is traditional, including fluffy turnips, cranberry sauce, giblet gravy, mashed potatoes. We do not, however, have the mince and apple pies. This is a sign of the times, for the children count calories and prefer to use them up on the main dinner. The small ones have dishes of ice cream while the adults have a fruit bowl, cheese, and crackers.

Toward evening, everyone is ready for cold turkey and thinly sliced dressing for sandwiches. It is self-service, for Mama is through for the day! Later we get out the corn popper and a bowl of apples, in case anyone is starving. We like corn popped in a rusty old popper from the early days, shaken back and forth over the embers in the fireplace.

When Thanksgiving is over, Christmas is hard at hand—in fact I wish, at times, there could be just one more week between them. I have for years and years promised myself that I would plan so as to be fresh and rested when Christmas comes, but it seems I have just gotten the turkey soup frozen (how Don loves that soup "with things in it") when it is time to put up the tree.

I remember when turkey was a once-in-a-year dinner. It symbolized Thanksgiving. Ham was for Easter, along with eggs cooked in fancy ways. Roast beef and Yorkshire pudding meant Christmas in our house when I was growing up, or stuffed goose when Mama could get it.

Our turkey came to town from a farm near Black Creek, I believe, and I stood around waiting to see Father bring it into the house. Then that delicious smell of sage and onion and savory filled the house as Mama stuffed his majesty and tucked him in the gas oven.

We were in Wisconsin, with the relatives in New England, so a family gathering was out of the question, but Mama had a housefull, as usual—the family doctor and his wife, a couple of homesick students from the college, a couple of single members of the faculty. All the leaves were put in the big mahogany table and the great lace cloth laid on. Father always said a hurried gruff blessing, for it embarrassed him to talk publicly to God. He addressed Him in private rather as one equal to another, but at the dinner table he flushed and ran the words together.

Nowadays turkey is so available it is no longer a seasonal treat. At times I am sorry it is so common, for that first thrill of seeing it on Thanksgiving morning is gone. The grandchildren accept turkey as just another good meal. I won't go so far as to say it should be restricted to holidays, but a few things should still be rare treats, I think. Of course it is always a treat to me because, since I live alone, the only turkey I meet is when the children assemble for a weekend or a holiday. One person, even with the help of an Irish and cockers, cannot undertake even a small turkey. The half-turkeys now available are fine for apartment dwellers but still too much for me.

An A"Maize"ingly Tasty Treat

Beverly Rae Wiersum

What is white and fluffy; light, and not stuffy; crunchy, often squeaky; and, in its undeveloped form, reminds one of a card game? Popcorn! This tasty treat titillates the tastebuds of millions of people around the world who agree that its delicious flavor is well worth crunching through the few "old maids" at the bottom of the bowl. For many years popcorn has been one of America's favorite snacks, but just where did this explosive treat originate?

Centuries before the first white man embarked upon a voyage to the New World, the natives of America had discovered the value of corn, or maize, as they called it. An excellent source of food, it could be grown easily, prepared in a variety of ways, and stored easily. The establishment of the first permanent white settlement in the New World depended on this golden grain. If Captain John Smith and the other colonists at Jamestown had not traded with the Indians for corn, they could never have escaped famine and starvation. Likewise, the Pilgrims survived their first harsh Massachusetts winter through the generosity of the Indians, who shared their stores of corn.

The Indians extended this generosity further, by teaching the colonists how to plant, cultivate, and harvest corn. They also showed them how to preserve the best seeds for future planting, and demonstrated the many ways in which corn could be prepared for eating and for feeding livestock.

Through these experiences, a warm friendship developed between the Pilgrims and the Indians. Gradually, popcorn, introduced to the colonists at the first Thanksgiving meal, came to be a sign of peace and a token of goodwill between the two peoples.

Farmers continued the tradition of growing popcorn for home use throughout the next two centuries and popcorn became commercialized in 1885 when the first steam-powered popping machine was invented. Mounted on wheels, it could go anywhere. Poppers soon appeared on street corners, at political rallies, fairs, band concerts, circuses, and outdoor gatherings of all kinds.

Popcorn and movies have always gone hand-in-hand, but early theater goers considered the crunchy, noisy, and messy food distracting. Theaters banned popcorn sales, but this did not stop vendors from setting up right outside the buildings. During the depression-ridden 1930s theater attendance suffered a severe decrease. In an effort to bring business back, theater operators reluctantly conceded, allowing vendors to set up concession stands (appropriately named) in their lobbies. Ironically, any theater without a concession stand continued to lose business. Apparently, the customers had changed their minds about the inconvenience of popcorn.

At the end of the 1940s, movie attendance and popcorn sales declined again as television began to take its toll. The leaders of the Popcorn Institute decided that the

solution to their problem was the revival of a centuries-old custom—popping corn at home. They launched an all-out campaign to persuade other companies to promote popcorn along with their products. Soon companies selling everything from soft drinks to salad oil began to promote popcorn along with their products and the sale of unpopped corn climbed. By 1952, the popcorn business reached a new peak.

Today, nearly everyone owns some sort of popper to make delicious popcorn at home, comparable to that sold in theaters. Well, not quite comparable. But homemade or theater-made, popcorn is still the same treat that the Indians enjoyed thousands of years ago. Although the technique of making it might be a bit more sophisticated than in the past, its simple goodness and delicious taste have remained the same. A treat even more American than Mom's apple pie, popcorn is definitely here to stay.

A TRADITIONAL THANKSGIVING

An Author's Thanksgiving

Thoughts on Autumn

Nathaniel Hawthorne

Still later in the season Nature's tenderness waxes stronger. It is impossible not to be fond of our mother now; for she is so fond of us! At other periods she does not make this impression on me, or only at rare intervals; but in these genial days of autumn, when she has perfected her harvests and accomplished every needful thing that was given her to do, then she overflows with a blessed superfluity of love. She has leisure to caress her children now. It is good to be alive at such times. Thank Heaven for breath—yes, for mere breath—when it is made up of a heavenly breeze like this! It comes with a real kiss upon our cheeks; it would linger fondly around us if it might; but since it must be gone, it embraces us with its whole kindly heart and passes onward to embrace likewise the next thing that it meets. A blessing is flung abroad and scattered far and wide over the earth, to be gathered up by all who choose. I recline upon the still unwithered grass and whisper to myself, "O perfect day! O beautiful world! O beneficent God!" And it is the promise of a blessed eternity; for our Creator would never have made such lovely days and have given us the deep hearts to enjoy them, above and beyond all thought, unless we were meant to be immortal. This sunshine is the golden pledge thereof. It beams through the gates of paradise and shows us glimpses far inward.

A New England Thanksgiving

The following is from an account of Thanksgiving dinner written in 1779 by Juliana Smith of Massachusetts in a letter to her cousin, Betsey. Juliana copied the letter into her diary, a common practice that guaranteed carefully written letters would not be lost in transmission. Juliana's diary was discovered by her descendant, Helen Everston Smith.

This year it was Uncle Simeon's turn to have the dinner at his house, but of course we all helped them as they help us when it is our turn, and there is always enough for us all to do. All the baking of pies and cakes was done at our house and we had the big oven heated and filled twice each day for three days before it was all done, and *everything was good*, though we did have to do without some things that ought to be used.

There was no Plumb Pudding, but a boiled Suet Pudding, stirred thick with dried Plumbs and Cherries, was called by the old Name and answered the purpose. All the other spice had been used in the Mince Pies, so for this Pudding we used a jar of West India preserved Ginger which chanced to be left of the last shipment which Uncle Simeon had from there, we chopped the Ginger small and stirred it through with the Plumbs and Cherries. It was extraordinarily good. The Day was bitter cold and when we got home from Meeting, which Father did not keep over long by reason of the cold, we were glad eno' of the fire in Uncle's Dining Hall, but by the time the dinner was one-half over those of us who were on the fire side of one Table were forced to get up and carry our plates with us around to the far side of the other Table, while those who had sat there were glad to bring their plates around to the fire side to get warm. All but the Old Ladies who had a screen put behind their chairs.

Uncle Simon was in his best mood, and you know how good that is! He kept both Tables in a roar of laughter with his droll stories of the days when he was studying medicine in Edinborough, and afterwards he and Father and Uncle Paul joined in singing Hymns and Ballads. You know how fine their voices go together. Then we all sang a Hymn and afterwards my dear Father led us in prayer, remembering all Absent Friends before the Throne of Grace, and much I wished that my dear Betsey was here as one of us, as she has been of yore.

We did not rise from the Table until it was quite dark, and then when the dishes had been cleared away we all got round the fire as close as we could, and cracked nuts, and sang songs and told stories. At least some told and others listened. You know nobody can exceed the two Grandmothers at telling tales of all the things they have seen themselves, and repeating those of the early years in New England, and even some in the Old England, which they had heard in their youth from their Elders. My Father says it is a goodly custom to hand down all worthy deeds and traditions from Father to Son, as the Israelites were commanded to do about Passover and as the Indians here have always done, because the Word that is spoken is remembered longer than the one that is written.

Traditions

Helen Colwell Oakley

The country Thanksgiving memories that I treasure most always include my mother in a pretty flowered house dress topped with a large, white bib-style apron, her hair in a bun and her cheeks a rosy pink as she bustled around our country kitchen preparing our Thanksgiving feast, continuing some of the holiday traditions started by her mother. Thanksgiving and Christmas were extra special holidays for farm children because the attics, cellars, sheds, and pantries were spilling over with the year's harvest. This gave a sense of security to the youngsters as well as the grown-ups; pickings were often slim before the harvest began. With every new harvest, we replenished our supplies, and our new bounty made Thanksgiving and Christmas even more memorable by the traditional feast which included foods we had only once a year. Since food is more plentiful today and festive dinners with roast turkey and ham appear more frequently on menus, we often must strive to make Thanksgiving traditions which are special.

Down on the farm where I live today we don't mind the extras which keep Thanksgivings as special as they were in Mom's day. We reserve roast turkey, dressing, and all of the trimmings for our Thanksgiving Day feast. Thanksgiving is still a family day, with all the kinfolk gathered around a large dining room table to give special thanks for our most bountiful feast of the year. Much of our food is still raised on the farm, keeping us aware of how blessed we are to have it. I find myself following in my mother's footsteps as we carry on the holiday traditions which Mom's family had passed down to her. I treasure them, and my daughter has discovered that she, too, must observe Thanksgiving traditions the way her own mother has always done.

For a time, we went modern down on the farm—out went the old wood stoves, pantries, butter churns, rocking chairs, and most anything that was classified as old-fashioned. Since then, many of us have come to our senses and long for a cozy country kitchen. Now we have a kitchen more like Mom's to prepare this year's Thanksgiving Day feast. I want my Thanksgiving to be memorable and traditional with a black wood stove to hover over as I cook the same old-fashioned specialties my mother did. By following these long-established traditions, we've found the secret to a perfect Thanksgiving, an old-fashioned holiday observation—with a dash or two of modernity—which is a happy combination of new and old traditions to please us all.

Late November

Lansing Christman

Thanksgiving is a festive day indoors and out. Families gather around teeming tables to express heartfelt thanks for what the land has yielded in its season of fruition. Though the hills are brown and sere, for those who follow the wonders of nature, there is a loveliness that brightens the holiday with lingering hues of red and gold.

On thin hillsides and in abandoned fields, after the rusty golden leaves of witch hazel have fluttered to the ground, the small trees are filled with yellow blooms which spread out feathery and ribbon-like among slender boughs. Seed pods of a year ago still cling to the branches, ready to explode with such force that the nuts are scattered many feet from the tree.

Some of the dandelions lift up their bowls of gold, defying frost and freeze as they reach for sunlight deep in the grass. The clustered orange berries of bittersweet cover the vines that twist and twine as they cling to old stone walls. Chickweed shows its tiny stars of white in the garden's edge.

In swamps and marshes, the bright red berries of black alder, a member of the holly family, spread splendor against a background of withered fields that reach up into the hills from a gentle stream flowing among the reeds and cattails. There, in the channel of the sluggish waters, muskrats build their houses of mud and sticks and roots. Alder berries set the swamp aglow in cloud or sun. Often glazed in ice from freezing rains, the berries, in their silvered sheen, shine and glow, cheering and warming the heart and spirit of a walker by the shore.

Nature helps light the way to a deeper understanding of harvest's end and of what God has given to humankind. We sing our praises of gratitude for His providence, for the goodness of the seasons, and for home and hills.

Thanksgiving Day is one of the last stepping stones from autumn into a wondrous world of white, when the earth takes its winter of rest under snow. Nature is like a mother tucking her child under the blankets when bedtime falls. And late November, with shortened hours of sunlight, turns the lamps low, and the land begins a long night of sleep.

Thanksgiving: Past Imperfect

Pamela Kennedy

We recently moved away from kith and kin and have relocated in a community hundreds of miles from anywhere we'd ever been before. When Thanksgiving came around, we were invited by some new friends to join them and several other upwardly-mobile young couples for a holiday dinner—adults only.

It was an evening to remember. The table was set with an exquisite arrangement of spicy gold chrysanthemums and autumn leaves. Bone china and lead crystal gleamed between flatware of shimmering sterling. Crisp linen underlined the settings and crowned each plate. In the serene glow of flickering tapers, we dined on a gourmet menu which included chilled cream of broccoli soup, cornish game hens in nests of wild rice, artichoke hearts vinaigrette and—the grand finale—praline bananas en flambe. It was utterly perfect—too perfect. In fact, it was hardly recognizable as Thanksgiving.

For me, Thanksgiving has always been a holiday full of family, confusion, craziness, and characters. It's the one holiday based on two principles that defy packaging or perfection. The whole day revolves around gratitude and eating—not necessarily in that order. We're talking about the basics here, and when a family gathers together and gets down to basics, strange things happen.

First of all, there are always more people than room. This means innovative seating arrangements must be devised. We always started with a large sheet of plywood on top of the dining room table. This usually created as many problems as it solved. We could seat extra folks, but the tablecloths never quite fit and the table was so wide and long, it was difficult to reach things. Then there was the droop factor. If the plywood was much larger than the table top, it took on a sort of convex appearance where the edges were a bit lower than the center. This was all right until Uncle Fred decided to hunker down with both elbows to get a better purchase on a drumstick. On one such occasion, the creamed onions gave into gravity and slid gracefully into Grandma's lap.

Children were always a prerequisite at Thanksgiving. If they were under two they were usually perched on telephone books or in high chairs next to a tolerant relative in washable clothes. From this vantage, the little darlings could, and usually did, pitch everything from salad to creamed peas with alarming accuracy. EFO's (edible flying objects) were always a part of every Thanksgiving I can recall.

If you were over two, but under fourteen, you were obliged to occupy a card table. One leg always threatened to cave in if nudged properly. The best thing about being at a card table, however, was the location, usually in the living room or a spare bedroom and out of earshot of any adults. You could burp, reach across the table, stick pitted olives on all ten fingers, or tell a joke with equal impunity. Someone always got the giggles right after taking a drink of milk and, depending upon the degree of muscle control, more or less saturated things. It was great! "Tell us the one about the school teacher with the hives again, Harold!"

Table settings were eclectic. No one knew it was called that, but that's what it was. Whoever had enough dishes and silverware for twenty-five people? The grown-ups got the good things that matched. The older children got the everyday stuff, but might end up with a salad fork and a tablespoon because the regular size was used up. Little people got divided plastic picnic plates and plastic glasses. The only crystal around was in Aunt Edna's brooch. The "good silver" really wasn't. It was plate, in a pattern called Queen Anne's Lace, and had been purchased with an astronomical number of Betty Crocker coupons.

The Thanksgiving menu was fairly predictable: turkey, candied sweet potatoes, mashed potatoes and gravy, creamed onions, peas and carrots, a fruit salad, dressing, relishes, and pies for dessert. Lots of pies. Everyone brought part of the dinner and it was assembled at the host's home. This usually made for some interesting developments—like the year Aunt Mildred's individual gelatin turkeys melted in the back seat during a traffic jam. I won't relate what the end product looked like, but Cousin Ellen's description made for great hilarity and lots of sprayed milk at one of the card tables.

Each relative had a "specialty" item, and it was prepared with great pride and received with appreciation—usually. Aunt Katie, however, always tried to be innovative. One year she experimented with horseradish in the aspic to "spice it up" as she said. She did a bang-up job! On another occasion she developed a variation of the classic perfection salad that henceforth was known as "Katie's imperfection."

The only time we ever had anything "en flambe" was the year Uncle Ben discovered a recipe in some magazine for doing the turkey in a brown paper bag. That was the same year we spent an hour trying to explain to Great-Grandma that we realized it wasn't traditional to have hot dogs on Thanksgiving.

Gratitude was always an integral part of our family gatherings and everyone was expected to share at least one blessing from the past year. Often, these testimonials were touching, sometimes heartwarming, always interesting and, on occasion, questionable. One that sticks in my memory was the year Uncle Harry rose solemnly, held up his water goblet, and intoned prayerfully, "I am extremely grateful that my beloved sister, Ada, has seen fit to spare us from her asparagus crepes this Thanksgiving." He sat down to a chorus of "Amens" and a patient sigh from Ada as she passed this year's offering, zucchini strata.

At our Thanksgiving dinners, the guests were as mismatched as the china. Uncle Richard, a nuclear engineer, chatted amicably with the young gas station attendant who had married one of the cousins. A first-time mother conferred with Great-Grandma about the ageless concerns of colic and cradle-cap. The children, all shapes and sizes, fit into all the niches—empty laps, empty corners, empty arms. It was a holiday that was warm, unstructured, and held together with the adhesive that binds us still—love.

Reflecting now upon it all, I must admit that my new friends' Thanksgiving was delicious and beautiful and wonderfully perfect. But I think if I could choose, I'd opt for my Thanksgivings—past-imperfect. For despite the chaos and confusion, they were always perfectly wonderful.

Autumn Time

Edgar A. Guest

One day in October I was puttering about my lawn when I heard on the street the almost human screech of grinding brakes. Hmm, I thought to myself, two Fords are about to kiss. I turned, expecting to see the tragedy, and was surprised to discover that sound had been produced by a single car. Then out of it began to pour the great crowd of people, which only a Ford can hold—the grandmother, the grandfather, the aunt, the uncle, the mother, and the children, and last of all, the father, who was the driver—and they arranged themselves into a group and began to admire a single tree ablaze in all the glory of fall.

It wasn't difficult to reconstruct what had taken place. Among them, I am sure it was the mother, was one with an eye to beauty. She had caught, through the little clear space allowed her, a flash of that scarlet foliage and had called excitedly to the father, "Stop!" I fancy he wondered what it was all about, but being dutiful he obeyed the command. And there they stood for a few minutes to admire that tree then closing its year of labor in a burst of beauty.

There was something about the incident that stayed with me. Men and women grow old and feeble, beauty deserts them, and at the end of their years so far as appearances go, they are at their very worst. Save the spiritual glow which comes from lives well lived, there is little about them to admire. I thought, wouldn't it be fine if we could come to the autumn time of our lives in splendor; if we could close our careers, keeping the admiration of all who have known us. And so that day this bit was done:

I want to come to autumn
    with the silver in my hair,
And maybe have the children stop
    to look at me and stare;
I'd like to reach October free
    from blemish or from taint,
As splendid as a maple tree
    which artists love to paint.

I'd like to come to autumn,
    with my life's work fully done
And look a little like a tree
    that's gleaming in the sun;
I'd like to think that I at last could
    come through care and tears
And be as fair to look upon
    as every elm appears.

But when I reach October,
    full contented I shall be
If those with whom I've walked through life
    shall still have faith in me;
Nor shall I dread the winter's frost,
    when brain and body tire,
If I have made my life a thing
    which others can admire.

How We Kept Thanksgiving at Oldtown

Abridged by Scott Giantvalley from Harriet Beecher Stowe's novel OLDTOWN FOLKS

People have often supposed, because the Puritans founded a society where there were no professed public amusements, that there was no fun going on, and that there were no cakes and ale, because Puritans were so virtuous. They were never more mistaken in their lives. There was an abundance of sober, well-considered merriment; but the king of all festivals was the autumn Thanksgiving.

When the apples were all gathered, the cider was all made, the yellow pumpkins were rolled in, the corn was husked, the labors of the season were done, and the warm, late days of Indian summer came in, dreamy and calm and still, with just enough frost to crisp the ground of a morning, but with warm traces of benign, sunny hours at noon, there came over the community a sort of genial repose of spirit, a sense of something accomplished, and of a new golden mark made on the calendar of life. The deacon began to say to the minister, of a Sunday, "I suppose it's about time for the Thanksgiving proclamation."

The glories of that proclamation! We knew beforehand the Sunday it was to be read, and the cheering anticipation sustained us through what seemed the long waste of the sermon and prayers. When at last the auspicious moment approached, we children poked one another, and fairly giggled with unreproved delight as we listened to the crackle of the slowly unfolding document. That great sheet of paper impressed us as something supernatural, by reason of its size, and by the broad seal of the state affixed thereto; and when the minister read, "By his excellency, the governor of the commonwealth of Massachusetts, a proclamation . . . " our mirth was with difficulty repressed by admonitory glances from our sympathetic elders. Then, after a solemn enumeration of the benefits which the commonwealth had that year received at the hands of Divine Providence, came at last the naming of the eventful day. And now came on the week in earnest!

During this eventful preparation week, all the female part of my grandmother's household were at a height above any ordinary state of mind; they moved about the house rapt in a species of prophetic frenzy. It seemed to be considered a necessary feature of such festivals, that everybody should be in a hurry, and everything in the house should be turned bottom upwards with enthusiasm; so at least we children understood it, and we certainly did our part to keep the ball rolling.

Well, at last, when all the chopping and pounding and baking and brewing, preparatory to the festival, were gone through with, the eventful day dawned. Great as the preparations were for the dinner, everything was so contrived that not a soul in the house should be kept from the morning service of Thanksgiving in the church and from listening to the Thanksgiving sermon. But it is to be confessed, that, when the good minister got carried away by the enthusiasm of his subject to extend these exercises beyond a certain length, anxious glances exchanged between good wives sometimes indicated a weakness of the flesh, having a tender reference to the turkeys and chickens and chicken pies, which might possibly be overdoing in the ovens at home.

When sermons and prayers were all over, we children rushed home to see the great feast of the year spread. What chitterings and chatterings there were all over the house, as the aunties, uncles and cousins came pouring in, taking off their things, looking at one another's bonnets and dresses, and mingling their comments on the morning sermon with various opinions on the new millinery outfits, and with bits of home news, and kindly neighborhood gossip.

Who shall do justice to the dinner and describe the turkey, chickens, and chicken pies with all that endless variety of vegetables which the American soil and climate have contributed to the table and which, without regard to the French doctrine of courses, were all piled together in a jovial abundance upon the board? There was much carving, laughing, talking and eating; and all showed that cheerful ability to dispatch the provisions which was the ruling spirit of the hour. After the meat came the plum puddings, and then the endless array of pies, till human nature was actually bewildered and overpowered by the tempting variety; and even we children turned from the profusion offered to us and wondered what was the matter that we could eat no more.

When all was over, my grandfather rose at the head of the table, and a fine venerable picture he made as he stood there, his silver hair flowing in curls down each side of his clear, calm face, while in conformity to the old Puritan custom, he called attention to a recital of the mercies of God in his dealings with the family; and then he gave out that psalm which in those days might be called the national hymn of the Puritans.

In the evening the house was all open and lighted with the best of tallow candles; it was understood that we were to have a dance, and the musician had rosined his bow and tuned his fiddle.

Whenever or wherever it was that the idea of the sinfulness of dancing arose in New England, I know not; it is a certain fact that at Oldtown, at this time, the presence of the minister and his lady was held not to be in the slightest degree incompatible with this amusement. Of course the dances in those days were of a strictly moral nature. The very thought of one of the dances of modern times would have sent Lady Lothrop behind her big fan in helpless confusion and exploded my grandmother like a full-charged arsenal of indignation. As it was, she stood, her broad pleased face radiant with satisfaction, as the wave of joyousness crept up higher and higher round her, till the elders, who stood keeping time with their heads and feet, began to tell one another how they had danced with their sweethearts in good old days gone by; and the elder women began to blush and boast of steps that they could take in their youth, till the music finally subdued them, and into the dance they went.

As nine o'clock struck, the whole scene dissolved and melted; for what well-regulated village would think of carrying festivities beyond that hour?

And so ended our Thanksgiving at Oldtown.

A Time for Settling In

Carole McCray

By the time November has arrived in our area, the Laurel Mountains of Pennsylvania, we have gotten a peek at winter; the first snow has fallen, leaving a light dusting that resembles confectioner's sugar.

To ease ourselves into colder weather, we have already made preparations. We delight in the stored autumn harvest. Quart and pint jars line canning shelves: a medley of pickles, beets, relishes, golden peaches, and stewed tomatoes is keeping company with homemade ketchup and tomato juice. Spicy applesauce and assorted jams and jellies have been put by, and the freezer holds blackberries, blueberries, and raspberries.

Bottled herbal vinegars sit on the old pine cupboard's shelves. We can choose from bottles of oregano, chive, and thyme, or purple basil vinegars.

In addition to herbal vinegars, we have also harvested and dried culinary herbs. During the summer months, we gathered herbs, and then tied and hung them upside down to dry. Now they have been preserved and labeled in glass containers covered with circles of gingham fabric and secured with grosgrain ribbons. When a low, sullen sky brings snowflakes whirling our way, our appetites develop a zest for robust meals. That is the time for hearty stews and simmering soups, flavored with basil, thyme, savory, and oregano.

Now that the herbs are dry and the holiday season is here, I like to make bouquet garni for friends. It is easy to do and is especially welcome for the cook who delights in unique seasonings. Three herbs—bay leaf, thyme, and parsley—are dried and crumbled and placed together in a four-inch square of cheesecloth. All the edges of the cheesecloth are brought together and secured with a string.

The advancement of winter in our community means preparing food for the birds, as well. We fill our bird feeders, and the black-capped chickadees return once more. I marvel at their fortitude! When the wind blows gusts of snow, these tiny creatures will peck away at the suet and fly to the feeder in sub-zero temperatures.

The return to the hearth is natural in winter; we are ready for crackling fires in the fireplace. Soon smoke is seen curling from chimneys, and the scent of wood smoke pervades the chilling air.

November can be a month of melancholy moods. But the Thanksgiving holiday arrives and lifts our spirits. We need a time of gathering and celebrating in November when a bleakness falls on the landscape. Not all November days are dark and raw; the mornings can awaken us to the surprise of azure skies and crisp days. The wet, windy days are balanced with Indian summer weather calling us to gather bittersweet bouquets, set the harvest table, and invite friends for a savory country supper. And because of our preparations, we are ready.

A Religious Thanksgiving

Psalm 100

Make a joyful noise unto the Lord, all ye lands.
Serve the Lord with gladness:
   come before his presence with singing.
Know ye that the Lord he is God;
   it is he that hath made us,
      and not we ourselves;
We are his people, and the sheep of his pasture.
Enter into his gates with thanksgiving,
   and into his courts with praise:
      be thankful unto him and bless his name.
For the Lord is good; his mercy is everlasting;
   and his truth endureth to all generations.

Thankful for This Day

Joy Belle Burgess

Across the hills, across the land,
A hymn of gratitude and praise
Resounds from every heart and woodland grove,
As we count our blessings, as we marvel at this autumn day!

Let us know the joy of living . . .

When earth's rich harvest lies before us
A splendor to behold,
When loved ones are around us
And we have a wealth more durable than gold,
When our hearts are filled with gratitude
For blessings untold,
When we can clasp another's hand
And lead him in from the cold.

Let us know the joy of living . . .

When the hills are vibrant and alive,
Clad in a bright array,
When flaming crimson and brilliant gold
Light up a hill's pathway,
When autumn casts her amber glow
To cheer and brighten our day,
When she sees our summer flowers,
Nipped by the frost, slowly fade away.

Across the hills, across the land,
Let us sing our hymn of praise,
For God hath shed His glorious light
On this most golden of His days!

We Gather Together

TRANSLATED FROM THE DUTCH

ARRANGED BY EDWARD KREMSER

1. We gath-er to-geth-er to ask the Lord's bless-ing;
2. Be-side us to guide us, our God with us join-ing,
3. We all do ex-tol Thee, Thou Lead-er tri-um-phant,

He chas-tens and has-tens His will to make known;
Or-dain-ing, main-tain-ing His king-dom di-vine;
And pray that Thou still our De-fend-er wilt be.

The wick-ed op-press-ing now cease from dis-tress-ing;
So from the be-gin-ning the fight we were win-ning;
Let Thy con-gre-ga-tion es-cape trib-u-la-tion;

Sing prais-es to His Name, He for-gets not His own.
Thou, Lord, wast at our side, all glo-ry be Thine.
Thy Name be ev-er praised! O Lord, Make us free! A-men.

Just Thinking

Author Unknown

Thankfulness is our crowning glory. The soul untouched by this emotion is without the quickening power which marks the difference between life and death. We must bring the fruitage of a happy, grateful soul to the throne of God, or else we come before Him empty-handed.

If we come not with smiles of grateful appreciation, we walk in darkness. If we carry no share of another's burden, we may still be weighted with a crushing load. If we lend no hand to a fellow wayfarer, we grope in vain for friendship. If we step not aside to give a firmer footing to a fallen brother, we fetter our own feet.

Now Thank We All Our God

MARTIN RINKART

JOHANN CRUGER

1. Now thank we all our God With heart and hands and voic - es,
2. O may this boun-teous God Through all our life be near us,
3. All praise and thanks to God The Fa - ther now be giv - en,

Who won-drous things hath done, In whom His world re - joic - es;
With ev - er joy - ful hearts And bless - ed peace to cheer us;
The Son, and Him who reigns With them in high - est heav - en,

Who, from our moth-er's arms, Hath blessed us on our way
And keep us in His grace And guide us when per - plexed,
The one e - ter - nal God Whom earth and heav'n a - dore;

With count - less gifts of love, And still is ours to - day.
And free us from all ills In this world and the next.
For thus it was, is now, And shall be ev - er - more.

Psalm 95

O Come, let us sing unto the Lord;
    let us make a joyful noise to the rock of our salvation.
Let us come before his presence with thanksgiving,
    and make a joyful noise unto him with psalms.
For the Lord is a great God, and a great King above all gods.
In his hand are the deep places of the earth:
    the strength of the hills is his also.
The sea is his, and he made it:
    and his hands formed the dry land.
O come, let us worship and bow down:
    let us kneel before the Lord our maker.
For he is our God; and we are the people of his pasture,
    and the sheep of his hand.

Thanksgiving Time

Elisabeth Weaver Winstead

November leaves come tumbling down
To sweep the cloud-gray sky.
And from the empty cornfield rows,
The bronze-tipped pheasants fly.

Gold pears adorn the orchard trees,
And squash reflects gold days.
Ripe apples gleam in shining bowls,
Near hearth fires all ablaze.

Large pumpkins line the roadside patch,
The barn holds fragrant hay.
We thank our God for nature's gifts,
Given to us this day.

This treasured harvest feast we share
With those we cherish best;
With happy hearts, we bow our heads
In gratitude expressed.

A RELIGIOUS THANKSGIVING

First Thanksgiving Day

TRADITIONAL

On the first Thanks - giv - ing Day, Pil - grims went to church to pray,
On the first Thanks - giv - ing Day, Pil - grims bowed their heads to pray,

Thanked the Lord for sun and rain, Thanked Him for the fields of grain.
Thanked the Lord for food to share, Thanked Him for a day so fair.

Now Thanks - giv - ing comes a - gain: Praise the Lord as they did then;
Now Thanks - giv - ing comes a - gain: Praise the Lord as they did then;

Thank Him for the sun and rain, Thank Him for the fields of grain.
Thank Him for our food to share, Thank Him for a day so fair.

A RELIGIOUS THANKSGIVING

Thanksgiving Today

Thanksgiving Day in the Morning

Aileen Fisher

What is the place you like the best
Thanksgiving Day in the morning?
The kitchen! With so many things to test,
And help to measure, and stir with zest,
And sniff and sample and all the rest—
Thanksgiving Day in the morning.

What are the colors you like the most
Thanksgiving Day in the morning?
The color of cranberries uppermost,
The pumpkin-yellow the pie tops boast,
The turkey-brown of a crispy roast—
Thanksgiving Day in the morning.

What are the sounds you think are gay
Thanksgiving Day in the morning?
The sizzly sounds on the roaster tray,
The gravy gurgling itself away,
The company sounds at the door—hooray!
Thanksgiving Day in the morning.

American Samplers

Historians have learned a lot over the years about the passengers of the *Mayflower*, but not much is known about their personal possessions. It seems certain, however, that the twenty-four women on the passenger list carried with them their sewing samplers and may even have passed the time on that dreary voyage improving their stitches.

The sampler of the colonial period, a narrow linen strip, was used by the owner to record her techniques in the cross-stitch, the drawn-work, faggot stitch, petit point, dam, and the other fancy stitches which she might later want to study before attempting their use in the decoration of linens and wearing apparel. The sampler, literally "a sample of stitches," was no new thing even at that time, its origin dating back to the time of Chaucer, when they were known as *ensemplers*.

The earliest existing sampler produced in America was made by Loara Standish, the daughter of Captain Myles Standish, military leader of the new colony at Plymouth. On her long linen strip Loara sewed wide bands of geometrical and floral designs with home-dyed thread using eyelet, satin, buttonhole, chain, outline, and cross-stitches. At the bottom of her sampler she inscribed, with yellow and blue thread, "Loara Standish is my name" and below this, being a pious Pilgrim girl, she further stitched:

Lord Guide my heart that I may do Thy will
And fill my heart with such convenient skill
As will conduce to Virtue void of Shame
And I will give the Glory to Thy Name.

This first American sampler is typical of the period, being the product of a mature needle-woman, and its inscriptions and devices were to be models for many more to follow.

With the beginning of the eighteenth century came changes in the production of samplers. The improved looms of the time turned out a much wider cloth and the samplers changed from long narrow strips to wider, more nearly square pieces. The change in shape brought with it a change in design element. Borders became the norm and greater unity was achieved in the decorative effect. Another change of this period was the change in age of the makers of the pieces. Before this time mature women had produced the sampler, but now they became the work of young girls, the showpiece which the girl produced to demonstrate her proficiency with the needle.

The needlework pictures, used to adorn the samplers, covered every conceivable subject from portraits and contemporary buildings, to pastoral scenes and Adam and Eve. The latter were usually modestly hidden behind enormous fig leaves and one prudish little girl even clothed this shame-free couple in Quaker costumes with Cain and Abel neatly stitched in knee breeches.

The verses that the girls chose ran heavily to piety and goodness, praise of parents, praise of beauty and nature, and verse mourning the loss of kinfolk. In the welter of goodness and piety one inscription stands out for its vigor and honesty. It reads, "Patty Polk did this and she hated every stitch she did in it. She loves to read much more."

During the last part of the eighteenth century and the first of the nineteenth the sampler makers began to include genealogical data on their work. Usually the names of the parents with their birth dates were recorded followed by the names and dates of all their children. The date of the death of any member of the family was stitched in later. Some samplers carry back to include the grandparents. Genealogists have found these samplers to be almost as useful as the old family Bible for tracing the family tree.

After the Civil War the making of samplers began gradually to die out, though a few still appear now and then in the needlework section at the county fairs. Collectors, decorators, and museums have taken up the sampler and there is a fairly brisk trade in them. Some of these collectors specialize in particular kinds of samplers, such as the all-white samplers or those of a particular period. The prices paid for samplers are not, however, in the same class with rare books, or old violins, so if you should find an authentic old sampler in your attic do not expect it to pay off the mortgage; you will probably find that its greatest value is in your own home as a cherished decoration.

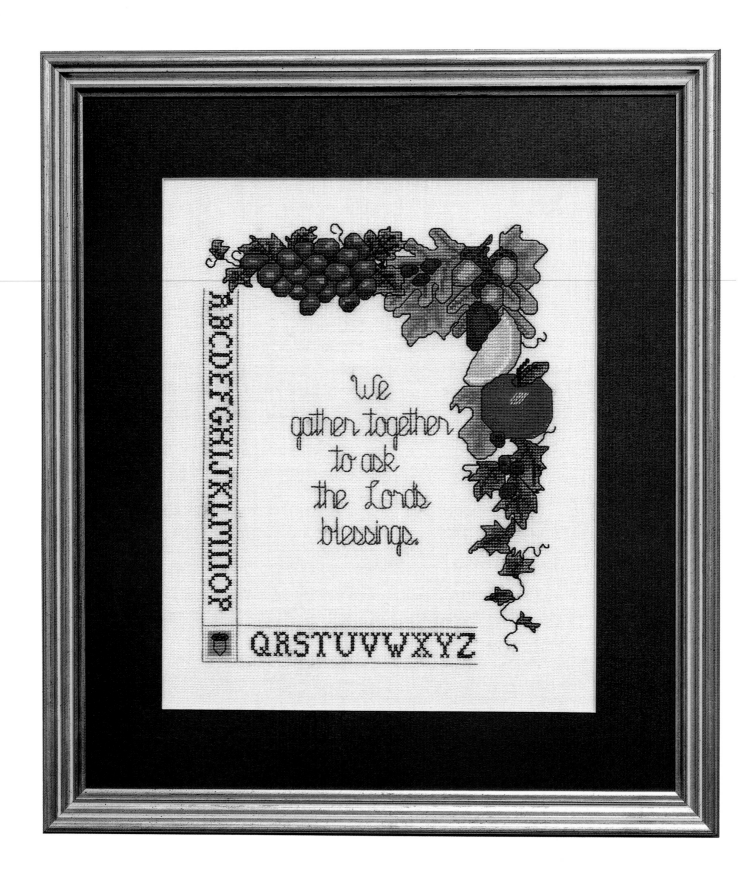

"Thanksgiving Blessings": A Cross-Stitch Sampler

Counted cross-stitch samplers provide beautiful accents for our homes as they convey the messages of our hearts. Yet, despite the beauty and complexity of the finished product, counted cross-stitch is a craft requiring few tools, and even fewer "skills." If you can count, make an "X," and thread a needle, you can perform this subtle art. Our "Thanksgiving Blessings" sampler, complete with vibrant fall colors and a special Thanksgiving message, will provide hours of quiet enjoyment, and it has the makings of a treasured family heirloom. The sampler is stitched on cream-colored 32 count Belfast linen. (Alternate fabrics/counts listed below.)

FINISHED DESIGN SIZE: 9¾" x 8" (Length=156 stitches; Width=128 stitches)

FINISHED PROJECT SIZE: 12¾" x 11" (Note: Measurements include 3" on each side for framing allowances.)

MATERIALS NEEDED: 13¾" x 12" Belfast linen; embroidery needle; scissors; DMC thread (see color chart); embroidery hoop.

PREPARING FABRIC: Prevent ravelling by binding edges with masking tape or by machine-stitching ⅛" from all edges.

FINDING PATTERN AND FABRIC CENTERS: The horizontal and vertical centers of the pattern are indicated by arrows. The cross (+) indicates design center. To locate fabric center, fold fabric in half, forming a rectangle. Mark crease with pins or with a tailor's pen. Now fold rectangular shape into a square; mark creases as before. Open fabric flat and baste between pins/pen marks, dividing fabric into four quarters. Fabric center is located where basting stitches intersect.

CROSS-STITCHING: *Important*: Use two strands of thread and work all stitches over two horizontal and two vertical fabric threads.

Comparing design center and fabric center, begin stitching on largest, most prominent object of pattern. (We suggest starting with the apple.) After threading needle, begin counting blocks from design and fabric centers; count off the corresponding number of blocks to be left blank until design begins. Make first "X" by pulling thread through *wrong side* of fabric in lower left corner of block where first stitch is to be made. Leave ¾" excess thread dangling on underside of fabric. Carry needle *diagonally* across two fabric threads to opposite corner, inserting it through the fabric from front to back. (See Figure 1)

To complete "cross" make another stitch from the opposite corner, covering first stitch and securing dangling thread from behind. Continue as instructed, keeping all stitches uniform in size and shape. After making a few stitches, place fabric in embroidery hoop, keeping work area centered and pulled tight. Finish entire project in like fashion, changing thread colors as pattern indicates.

FINISHING TOUCHES: Reserve backstitching for last. (See Figure 2 and color chart for appropriate stitching method and colors.) If desired, backstitch your initials in finished design.

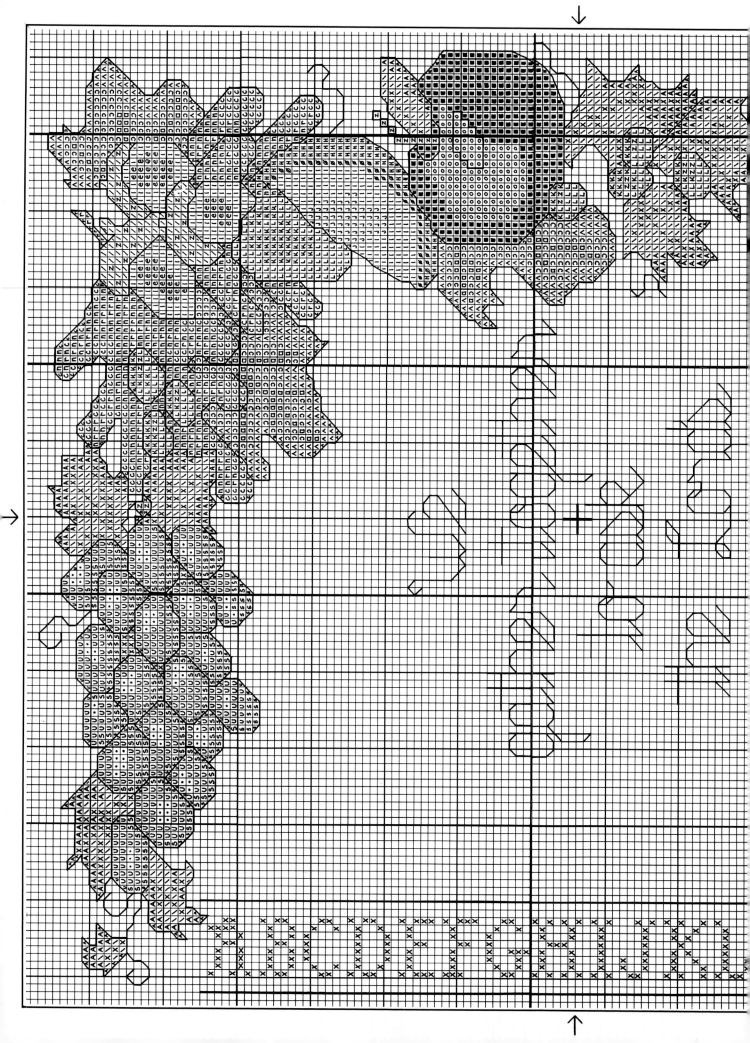

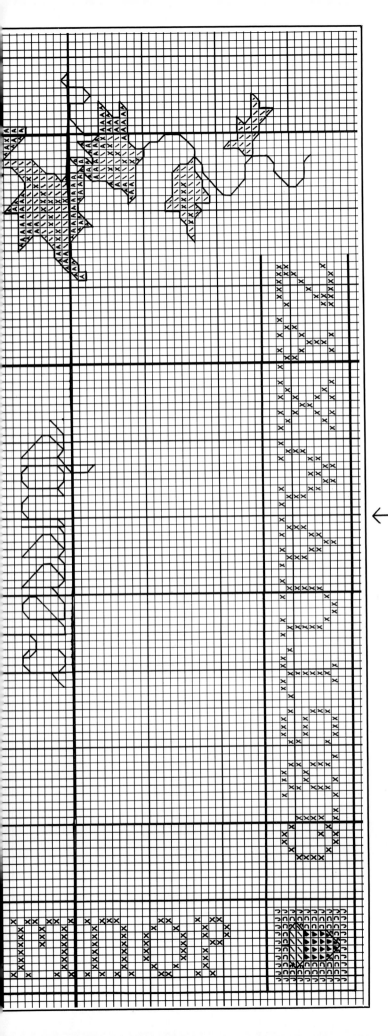

DMC COLORS

- ■ 304 Dark red
- ⊙ 321 Bright red
- ╱ 433 Dark brown
  (also backstitching for message)
- ▼ 435 Medium brown
  (also backstitching for alphabet border)
- ℮ 437 Light brown
- X 500 Dark green

- ╲ 501 Medium green
- ⋀ 502 Light green
- S 550 Dark purple
- U 552 Medium purple
- • 553 Light purple
- ☐ 720 Dark orange

- ⊂ 721 Medium orange
- ⋀ 722 Light orange
- H 741 Dark orange
- I 742 Medium orange
- J 743 Light orange
- K 815 Light red

- L 902 Dark red
- Z 938 Dark brown
  (all other backstitching)
- Γ 975 Dark brown
- ⊓ 976 Medium brown
- ⊂ 977 Light brown
- ∅ Ecru (also backstitching for apple)

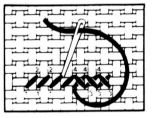

Figure 1

Figure 2

Fabric options:

aida	11ct	14 2/11	11 7/11
aida	14ct	11 1/7	9 1/7
aida	18ct	8 2/3	7 1/8
aida	22ct	7 1/11	5 9/11

THANKSGIVING TODAY

I Would Give Thanks

Virginia Katherine Oliver

I would give thanks for many things
On this Thanksgiving Day,
Thanks for all the blessings life brings
Each day along the way.

I would give thanks for life, for health,
For home, for food, and too,
All that I count my greatest wealth . . .
Family and friendship true.

I would give thanks for my native land,
For freedom on this day,
Where we worship and understand
Our privilege to pray.

I would give thanks for many things
And do the best I can
To be worthy of all life brings
And serve my fellow man.

A Modern Thanksgiving Dinner

Bonnie Aeschliman

Turkey Breast with Thyme Glaze

1   small fresh turkey breast
½   cup margarine
1   teaspoon dried thyme
¼   teaspoon pepper
2   cups chicken broth
3-4 tablespoons cornstarch
½   cup white wine or water

Preheat oven to 325°. Place turkey breast, skin side up, in a roasting pan. Roast turkey breast for 2½ hours, or until meat thermometer measures 170°. About 45 minutes before turkey is done, melt margarine over low heat. Stir in thyme, and pepper. Brush turkey with herb-butter mixture. Continue roasting, brushing frequently with herb-butter mixture until turkey is done.

Pour the pan drippings into a large measuring cup. Chill, then skim off fat. Add broth to make four cups. Return mixture to roasting pan and bring to a simmer over low heat, stirring constantly. Dissolve cornstarch in wine or water and stir until smooth. Add to drippings in roasting pan. Bring to a boil over medium heat, whisking constantly. Boil one minute. Spoon gravy over sliced turkey.

Artichoke Saute
Serves 4

3   artichokes
    Lemon juice
1   small onion, sliced
1   clove garlic, minced
2   tablespoons olive oil
1   teaspoon sugar
½   teaspoon dried tarragon
¼-½ cup water
    Pepper

1   cup sliced mushrooms
1   medium tomato, seeded and chopped

Wash artichokes and remove outer leaves. Continue to snap off and discard tops of the thick inner leaves until reaching center core of pale green leaves.

Cut off stems and top two inches of artichokes; discard. Cut artichokes in half lengthwise. Scrape out the fuzzy center; discard. Cut each artichoke half into fourths lengthwise. Rub with lemon juice.

Saute onion and garlic in olive oil until tender. Add artichokes, mushrooms, sugar, tarragon, and water. Simmer, stirring occasionally, for 10 to 15 minutes, or until artichokes are tender. Stir in tomato; simmer until tomato is thoroughly heated.

Pasta Pronto
Serves 4

3   green onions, chopped
1   clove garlic, minced
2   tablespoons olive oil
¾   cup light cream
2   tablespoons crushed fresh basil, or
    1 teaspoon dried basil
2   tablespoons crushed fresh parsley or
    1 teaspoon dried parsley
1   cup ripe olives
½   cup finely chopped walnuts
    Pepper
8   ounces fettucine type pasta, cooked
½   cup freshly grated Parmesan cheese

Saute onion and garlic in oil until tender; add cream, basil, and parsley. Bring to a boil; simmer until liquid is slightly reduced. Stir in olives, nuts, and pepper to taste. Pour over hot pasta and sprinkle with cheese; toss to mix.

THANKSGIVING TODAY

Pass the Persimmons, Please

Mildred Estes

*P*ersimmons are a neglected fruit, yet they have an elegant flavor and great possibilities. Granted, they are not the most beautiful fruit and they will pucker your mouth if eaten before ripe. But they are worth a taste, especially in the fall, when they are most readily available in the market produce section. They are delicious in cookies, pudding, salads, ice cream and bread.

In America, persimmons date back to the days of early explorers. DeSoto reported the presence of persimmons in the southern United States in the 1540s. Jan deLaet described the persimmon in his writings about Virginia in 1558. Persimmons were used by Indians as food and by early settlers in the Appalachian and Ozark highlands for persimmon bread, supposedly superior to gingerbread. The seeds, when roasted or ground, are used as a coffee substitute in the southern United States.

In the United States, there are two principle varieties of persimmons: the Oriental and the native American. The Oriental (native to central and northern China) grows primarily in the western states, California in particular. The native American variety can be found in the southern and eastern parts of the United States.

The Oriental variety (D. kaki) resembles a tomato in size and shape. The fruit may be up to three inches in diameter and is bright yellow to orange when ripe. If eaten before it is soft-ripe, it is unpleasantly astringent.

The native American persimmon tree (Diospyros, species D. virginiana), elegant and wide spreading may grow to seventy-five feet. The deep root system adapts to a wide range of soils. The fruit is triangular in shape, about three inches in diameter. It must be ripened by a hard frost which softens it, removing the astringency and developing a rich flavor. In the southern part of the United States, this variety is often found along fencerows around fields.

Either variety of persimmon may be frozen. To freeze, peel and place the whole fruit in a blender for pureeing. After blending, the pulp may be frozen by cupfuls in plastic bags. This frozen pulp keeps from one season to another without losing flavor.

If you wish to dry the whole fruit, the Hachiya, a variety of Oriental, is best. Peel the fruit while it is still firm and yet bright orange in color; do not cut up. Hang the fruit by the stem using a durable string or plastic cord. Be certain the area in which the fruit hangs is dry. After it has hung for several days, break up the fibers by lightly kneading the fruit. Continue doing this over the several weeks it takes to completely dry the persimmons. When ready to eat, the persimmon is wrinkled and resembles a prune.

In California, the Fuyu variety (Oriental) is popular for slicing and drying. Wash but do not peel the persimmons. Cut into 3/8-inch slices. Place in single layers on trays. Dry for 14 to 18 hours until hard, but still bendable. To reconstitute, place 1/2 cup of persimmon slices in a narrow, high-walled container so 1/2 cup of warm water will almost cover them. Soak overnight until soft. Eat as fresh.

Dried persimmons may be used in recipes without soaking if they are pureed in a blender with water.

Actually, the persimmon tree can claim good looks all year round. Neatly tailored leaves emerge in the spring and turn color in the fall; an interesting bare-branch pattern is visible in winter. Even the bark, with its checkerboard pattern, has a pleasing texture. The fruit hangs like Christmas ornaments for a number of weeks in the fall.

Even if you are not fortunate enough to have a persimmon tree yourself, don't shy away from the fruit in the produce section of your market. Make a resolution that this season you will, at the very least, try persimmons—sliced raw like apples, or in cookies, cake, or whatever use appeals to you. You may become a convert.

Persimmon Cookies

$\frac{1}{2}$ cup shortening
1 cup sugar
1 egg
2 cups flour
1 teaspoon ground cinnamon
$\frac{1}{2}$ teaspoon ground cloves
$\frac{1}{2}$ teaspoon nutmeg
$\frac{1}{2}$ teaspoon salt
1 teaspoon baking soda
1 cup persimmon pulp
1 cup raisins, dates, or prunes
1 cup chopped walnuts or pecans

Cream shortening and sugar. Add egg and beat well. In small bowl, combine flour, spices, salt, and baking soda. Stir flour mixture into creamed shortening mixture. Add persimmon pulp, raisins and nuts; mix well. Drop by spoonfuls, 2 inches apart onto lightly greased cookie sheet. Bake at 350° for 10 to 12 minutes. Makes 3 dozen.

Persimmon Ice Cream

1 cup sliced dried persimmons
1 cup water
$\frac{1}{4}$ teaspoon ground cinnamon
$\frac{1}{8}$ teaspoon each ground cloves and mace
$2\frac{1}{2}$ tablespoon fresh lemon juice
2 cups vanilla ice cream, softened.

Combine the first 5 ingredients in a blender until the mixture is the consistency of a thick sauce. Add lemon juice as needed. Pour the mixture over ice cream; blend well. Pour into freezing trays; chill until firm. Makes about 3 cups.

PHOTOGRAPHY AND ART CREDITS

Project Editor, Nancy J. Skarmeas; Associate Editor, Fran Morley;
Editorial Assistant, LaNita Kirby; Book Designer, Patrick McRae

B
C
D
E
F
G
H
I
J